To Nicole
Love Uncle Hugh + Aunt Linda

1998

W9-ABE-767

For my father, Archie Beck

What is the time?
Half-past pickaxe, quarter to shovel

If it takes a man a mile to walk a fortnight,
how many apples in a barrel of plums?

Rhymes and Songs
for the
Very Young

Ian Beck

BARNES
&NOBLE
BOOKS
NEW YORK

Illustrations © Ian Beck 1995

Selection and arrangement © Oxford University Press 1995

This U.S. Edition of *The Oxford Nursery Book* originally published in England in 1995 is
published by arrangement with Oxford University Press.

1996 Barnes & Noble Books

ISBN 0-76070-360-4

Printed and bound in Spain

M 9 8 7 6 5 4 3

Gráficas

Contents

Boys and Girls Come Out to Play

Boys and girls come out to play,
The moon doth shine as bright as day.
Leave your supper and leave your sleep,
And join your playfellows in the street.
Come with a whoop and come with a call,
Come with a good will or not at all.
Up the ladder and down the wall,
A half-penny loaf will serve us all;
You find milk and I'll find flour,
And we'll have a pudding in half an hour.

Round and Round the Garden

Round and round the garden
Like a teddy bear;
One step, two step,
Tickle you under there!

Row, Row, Row Your Boat

Row, row, row your boat,
Gently down the stream,
Merrily, merrily, merrily, merrily,
Life is but a dream.

I Saw a Ship A-Sailing

I saw a ship a-sailing,
A-sailing on the sea;
And oh! it was laden
With pretty things for me.

There was dried fruit in the cabin,
And apples in the hold;
The sails were made of silk,
And the masts were made of gold.

The four-and-twenty sailors
That stood between the decks,
Were four-and-twenty white mice,
With chains around their necks.

The Captain was a duck,
With a package on his back,
And when the ship began to move,
The Captain said, "Quack, quack!"

Humpty Dumpty

Humpty Dumpty sat on a wall,
Humpty Dumpty had a great fall:
All the King's horses and all the King's men
Couldn't put Humpty together again.

I Had a Little Nut-Tree

I had a little nut-tree,
Nothing would it bear
But a silver nutmeg
And a golden pear.

The King of Spain's daughter
Came to visit me,
And all for the sake
Of my little nut-tree.

I skipped over water,
I danced over sea,
And all the birds in the air
Couldn't catch me!

Little Bo-Peep

Little Bo-Peep has lost her sheep,
And doesn't know where to find them;
Leave them alone, and they'll come home,
Bringing their tails behind them.

Little Bo-Peep fell fast asleep,
And dreamed she heard them bleating;
But when she awoke, she found it a joke,
For they were still a-fleeting.

Then up she took her little crook,
Determined for to find them;
She found them indeed, but it made her heart bleed,
For they'd left their tails behind them.

It happened one day, as Bo-Peep did stray
Into a meadow nearby,
There she espied their tails side by side,
All hung on a tree to dry.

She heaved a sigh, and wiped her eye,
And ran o'er hill and dale-o,
And tried what she could, as a shepherdess
  should,
To tack to each sheep its tail-o.

A Cat Came Fiddling

A cat came fiddling out of a barn,
With a pair of bagpipes under her arm;
She could sing nothing but "Fiddle-de-dee.
The mouse has married the bumblebee."
Pipe, cat—dance, mouse—
We'll have a wedding at our good house.

The Herring

The herring loves the merry moonlight
And the mackerel loves the wind,
But the oyster loves the dredging song
For he comes of a gentle kind.

Way Down South

Way down South where bananas grow,
A grasshopper stepped on an elephant's toe.
The elephant said, with tears in his eyes,
"Pick on somebody your own size."

Alas! Alas! for Miss Mackay!

Alas! Alas! for Miss Mackay!
Her knives and forks have run away,
And when the cups and spoons are going,
She's sure there is no way of knowing.

Itsy Bitsy Spider

The Itsy Bitsy spider
Climbed up the water spout;

Down came the rain
And washed the spider out;

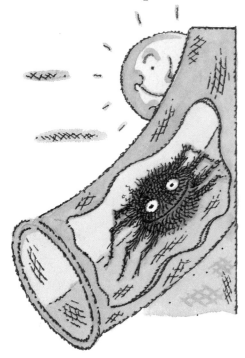

Out came the sun
And dried up all the rain;

And the Itsy Bitsy spider
Climbed up the spout again.

Hickory, Dickory, Dock

Hickory, dickory, dock,
The mouse ran up the clock.
The clock struck one,
The mouse ran down,
Hickory, dickory, dock.

I'm a Little Teapot

I'm a little teapot, short and stout,
Here is my handle,
Here is my spout.
When I get the steam up, hear me shout,
"Tip me over and pour me out."

Polly Put the Kettle On

Polly put the kettle on,
Polly put the kettle on,
Polly put the kettle on,
We'll all have tea.

Sukey take it off again,
Sukey take it off again,
Sukey take it off again,
They've all gone away.

25

Doctor Foster

Doctor Foster went to Gloucester
In a shower of rain.
He stepped in a puddle,
Right up to his middle,
And never went there again.

The Old Man with a Beard

There was an old man with a beard
Who said, "It is just as I feared!
Two owls and a hen,
Four larks and a wren,
Have all built their nests in my beard!"

Edward Lear

Three Wise Men

Three wise men of Gotham,
They went to sea in a bowl,
And if the bowl had been stronger,
My song had been longer.

Rub-a-Dub-Dub

Rub-a-dub-dub,
Three men in a tub,
And who do you think they were?
The butcher, the baker,
The candlestick-maker;
All going to the fair.

The Big Ship Sails on the Alley, Alley O

The big ship sails on the alley, alley O,
The alley, alley O, the alley, alley O.
The big ship sails on the alley, alley O,
On the last day of September.

The captain said, "It will never, never do,
Never never do, never never do."
The captain said, "It will never, never do,"
On the last day of September.

The big ship sank to the bottom of the sea,
The bottom of the sea, the bottom of the sea.
The big ship sank to the bottom of the sea,
On the last day of September.

We all dip our heads in the deep blue sea,
The deep blue sea, the deep blue sea.
We all dip our heads in the deep blue sea,
On the last day of September.

Jumping Joan

Here am I,
Little jumping Joan,
When nobody's with me,
I'm all alone.

Jack

Jack be nimble,
Jack be quick,
Jack jump over
The candlestick.

Teasing

Little Jack Horner sat in the corner
Eating his curds and whey.
There came a big spider,
Who sat down beside him,
And the dish ran away with the spoon.
Ha-Ha.

The Owl and the Pussycat

The Owl and the Pussycat went to sea
In a beautiful pea-green boat;
They took some honey, and plenty of money
Wrapped up in a five-pound note.
The Owl looked up to the stars above,
And sang to a small guitar,
"O lovely Pussy, O Pussy, my love,
What a beautiful Pussy you are,
You are,
You are!
What a beautiful pussy you are!"

34

Pussy said to the Owl, "You elegant fowl,
How charmingly sweet you sing!
Oh! let us be married; too long we have tarried:
But what shall we do for a ring?"
They sailed away, for a year and a day,
To the land where the bong-tree grows,
And there in a wood a Piggy-wig stood,
With a ring at the end of his nose,
His nose,
His nose,
With a ring at the end of his nose.

"Dear Pig, are you willing to sell for one shilling
Your ring?" Said the Piggy, "I will."
So they took it away, and were married next day
By the Turkey who lives on the hill.
They dined on mince and slices of quince,
Which they ate with a runcible spoon;
And hand in hand, on the edge of the sand,
They danced by the light of the moon,
The moon,
The moon,
They danced by the light of the moon.

Edward Lear

The Common Cormorant

The common cormorant or shag
Lays eggs inside a paper bag
The reason you will see no doubt
It is to keep the lightning out.
But what these unobservant birds
Have never noticed is that herds
Of wandering bears may come with buns
And steal the bags to hold the crumbs.

How Doth the Little Crocodile

How doth the little crocodile
Improve his shining tail,
And pour the waters of the Nile
On every golden scale!

How cheerfully he seems to grin,
How neatly spreads his claws,
And welcomes little fishes in,
With gently smiling jaws!

Lewis Carroll

If You Should Meet a Crocodile

If you should meet a crocodile,
Don't take a stick and poke him;
Ignore the welcome in his smile,
Be careful not to stroke him.
For as he sleeps upon the Nile,
He thinner gets and thinner;
But whene'er you meet a crocodile
He's ready for his dinner.

Higglety Pigglety

Higglety pigglety pop
The dog has eaten the mop
The pig's in a hurry
The cat's in a flurry
Higglety pigglety pop.

Twinkle, Twinkle, Little Bat

Twinkle, twinkle, little bat!
How I wonder what you're at?
Up above the world you fly,
Like a tea-tray in the sky.

Lewis Carroll

She Sells Seashells on the Seashore

She sells seashells on the seashore,
The shells she sells are seashells I'm sure.
So if she sells seashells on the seashore,
I'm sure the shells are seashore shells.

Round and Round the Rugged Rock

Round and round the rugged rock,
The ragged rascal ran.
How many R's are there in that?
Now tell me if you can.

Peter Piper

Peter Piper picked a peck of pickled peppers.
Did Peter Piper pick a peck of pickled peppers?
If Peter Piper picked a peck of pickled peppers,
Where's the peck of pickled peppers Peter Piper picked?

Little Bird of Paradise

Little bird of paradise,
She works her work both neat and nice;
She pleases God, she pleases man,
She does the work that no man can.

A Chimney

Black within, red without,
Four corners round about.

Snow

A milk-white bird
Floats down through the air.
And never a tree
But he lights there.

An Egg

In marble walls as white as milk,
Lined with a skin as soft as silk,
Within a fountain crystal-clear,
A golden apple doth appear.
No doors there are to this stronghold,
Yet thieves break in and steal the gold.

Star

Higher than a house,
Higher than a tree;
Oh, whatever can that be?

A Star

I have a little sister, they call her Peep-Peep,
She wades the waters deep, deep, deep;
She climbs the mountains high, high, high;
Poor little creature she has but one eye.

Cuckoo, Cuckoo

Cuckoo, cuckoo,
What do you do?
In April
I open my bill;
In May
I sing night and day;
In June
I change my tune;
In July
Away I fly;
In August
Away I must.

Rain

Rain on the green grass,
And rain on the tree,
Rain on the housetop,
But not on me.

The Sound of the Wind

The wind has such a rainy sound
Moaning through the town,
The sea has such a windy sound,
Will the ships go down?

The apples in the orchard
Tumble from their tree.
Oh will the ships go down, go down,
In the windy sea?

Christina Rossetti

Is the Moon Tired?

Is the moon tired? She looks so pale
Within her misty veil;
She scales the sky from east to west,
And takes no rest.

Before the coming of the night
The moon shows papery white;
Before the dawning of the day,
She fades away.

Christina Rossetti

Christmas

Christmas is coming
The goose is getting fat,
Please to put a penny
In the old man's hat.
If you haven't got a penny
A half-penny will do,
If you haven't got a half-penny,
God bless you.

We Wish You a Merry Christmas

We wish you a merry Christmas,
We wish you a merry Christmas,
We wish you a merry Christmas,
And a happy New Year.
Good tidings we bring
To you and your kin.
We wish you a merry Christmas
And a happy New Year.

Little Jack Horner

Little Jack Horner
Sat in a corner,
Eating a Christmas pie;
He put in his thumb,
And pulled out a plum,
And said, "What a good boy am I!"

The Twelve Days of Christmas

On the first day of Christmas,
My true love sent to me
A partridge in a pear tree.

On the second day of Christmas,
My true love sent to me
Two turtledoves, and
A partridge in a pear tree.

On the third day of Christmas,
My true love sent to me
Three French hens,
Two turtledoves, and
A partridge in a pear tree.

On the fourth day of Christmas,
My true love sent to me
Four colly birds,
Three French hens,
Two turtledoves, and
A partridge in a pear tree.

On the fifth day of Christmas,
My true love sent to me
Five gold rings,
Four colly birds,
Three French hens,
Two turtledoves, and
A partridge in a pear tree.

On the sixth day of Christmas,
My true love sent to me
Six geese a-laying,
Five gold rings,
Four colly birds,
Three French hens,
Two turtledoves, and
A partridge in a pear tree.

On the seventh day of Christmas,
My true love sent to me
Seven swans a-swimming,
Six geese a-laying,
Five gold rings,
Four colly birds,
Three French hens,
Two turtledoves, and
A partridge in a pear tree.

On the eighth day of Christmas,
My true love sent to me
Eight maids a-milking,
Seven swans a-swimming,
Six geese a-laying,
Five gold rings,
Four colly birds,
Three French hens,
Two turtledoves, and
A partridge in a pear tree.

On the ninth day of Christmas,
My true love sent to me
Nine drummers drumming,
Eight maids a-milking,
Seven swans a-swimming,
Six geese a-laying,
Five gold rings,
Four colly birds,
Three French hens,
Two turtledoves, and
A partridge in a pear tree.

On the tenth day of Christmas,
My true love sent to me
Ten pipers piping,
Nine drummers drumming,
Eight maids a-milking,
Seven swans a-swimming,
Six geese a-laying,
Five gold rings,
Four colly birds,
Three French hens,
Two turtledoves, and
A partridge in a pear tree.

On the eleventh day of Christmas,
My true love sent to me
Eleven ladies dancing,
Ten pipers piping,
Nine drummers drumming,
Eight maids a-milking,
Seven swans a-swimming,
Six geese a-laying,
Five gold rings,
Four colly birds,
Three French hens,
Two turtle doves, and
A partridge in a pear tree.

On the twelfth day of Christmas,
My true love sent to me
Twelve lords a-leaping,
Eleven ladies dancing,
Ten pipers piping,
Nine drummers drumming,
Eight maids a-milking,
Seven swans a-swimming,
Six geese a-laying,
Five gold rings,
Four colly birds,
Three French hens,
Two turtledoves, and
A partridge in a pear tree.

Jingle Bells

Dashing through the snow
In a one-horse open sleigh;
O'er the fields we go,
Laughing all the way.
Bells on bobtail ring,
Making spirits bright;
What fun it is to ride and sing
A sleighing song tonight!

Jingle bells, jingle bells,
Jingle all the way.
O! What fun it is to ride
In a one-horse open sleigh.

Jingle bells, jingle bells,
Jingle all the way.
O! What fun it is to ride
In a one-horse open sleigh.

I Saw Three Ships Come Sailing By

I saw three ships come sailing by,
Come sailing by, come sailing by,
I saw three ships come sailing by,
On Christmas Day in the morning.

And what do you think was in them then,
Was in them then, was in them then?
And what do you think was in them then,
On Christmas Day in the morning?

Three pretty girls were in them then,
Were in them then, were in them then,
Three pretty girls were in them then,
On Christmas Day in the morning.

One could whistle, and one could sing,
And one could play on the violin;
Such joy there was at my wedding,
On Christmas Day in the morning.

I Sing of a Maiden

I sing of a maiden
That is makeless;
King of all kings
To her son she chose.

He came all so still
There his mother was,
As dew in April
That falleth on the grass.

He came all so still
To his mother's bower,
As dew in April
That falleth on the flower.

He came all so still
There his mother lay,
As dew in April
That falleth on the spray.

Mother and maiden
Was never none but she;
Well may such a lady
God's mother be.

The Lamb

Little Lamb, who made thee?
Dost thou know who made thee?

Gave thee life, and bid thee feed
By the stream and o'er the mead;
Gave thee clothing of delight,
Softest clothing, woolly, bright;
Gave thee such a tender voice,
Making all the vales rejoice?

Little Lamb, who made thee?
Dost thou know who made thee?

Little Lamb, I'll tell thee,
Little Lamb, I'll tell thee:

He is called by thy name,
For He calls Himself a lamb.
He is meek, and He is mild;
He became a little child.
I a child, and thou a lamb,
We are called by His name.

Little Lamb, God bless thee!
Little Lamb, God bless thee!

William Blake

The Swing

How do you like to go up in a swing,
Up in the air so blue?
Oh, I do think it the pleasantest thing
Ever a child can do!

Up in the air and over the wall,
Till I can see so wide.
Rivers and trees and cattle and all
Over the countryside—

Till I look down on the garden green,
Down on the roof so brown—
Up in the air I go flying again,
Up in the air and down!

Robert Louis Stevenson

Horses

The horses of the sea
Rear a foaming crest,
But the horses of the land
Serve us the best.

The horses of the land,
Munch corn and clover,
While the foaming sea-horses
Toss and turn over.

Christina Rossetti

Boats Sail on the Rivers

Boats sail on the rivers,
And ships sail on the seas;
But clouds that sail across the sky
Are prettier far than these.

There are bridges on the rivers,
As pretty as you please;
But the bow that bridges heaven,
And overtops the trees,
And builds a road from earth to sky,
Is prettier far than these.

Christina Rossetti

Bed in Summer

In winter I get up at night
And dress by yellow candle-light.
In summer, quite the other way,
I have to go to bed by day.

I have to go to bed and see
The birds still hopping on the tree,
Or hear the grown-up people's feet
Still going past me in the street.

And does it not seem hard to you
When all the sky is clear and blue,
And I should like so much to play,
To have to go to bed by day?

Robert Louis Stevenson

Where Go the Boats?

Dark brown is the river,
Golden is the sand.
It flows along for ever,
With trees on either hand.

Green leaves a-floating,
Castles of the foam,
Boats of mine a-boating—
Where will all come home?

On goes the river
And out past the mill,
Away down the valley,
Away down the hill.

Away down the river,
A hundred miles or more,
Other little children
Shall bring my boats ashore.

Robert Louis Stevenson

At the Seaside

When I was down beside the sea
A wooden spade they gave to me
To dig the sandy shore.
My holes were empty like a cup,
In every hole the sea came up,
Till it could come no more.

Robert Louis Stevenson

Infant Joy

"I have no name;
"I am but two days old."
What shall I call thee?
"I happy am;
"Joy is my name."
Sweet joy befall thee!

Pretty joy!
Sweet joy but two days old,
Sweet joy I call thee.
Thou dost smile,
I sing the while.
Sweet joy befall thee!

William Blake

Night

The sun descending in the west,
The evening star does shine;
The birds are silent in their nest,
And I must seek for mine.
The moon, like a flower,
In heaven's high bower,
With silent delight
Sits and smiles on the night.

Farewell, green fields and happy groves,
Where flocks have took delight;
Where lambs have nibbled, silent moves
The feet of angels bright.
Unseen they pour blessing,
And joy without ceasing,
On each bud and blossom,
And each sleeping bosom.

William Blake

Sunset

The summer sun is sinking low;
Only the tree-tops redden and glow;
Only the weather-cock on the spire
Of the village church is a flame of fire;
All is in shadow below.

Henry Wadsworth Longfellow

African Lullaby

Sleep, sleep, my little one! The night is all wind and rain;
The meal has been wet by the raindrops and bent is the sugar cane;
O Giver who gives to the people, in safety my little son keep!
My little son with the headdress sleep, sleep, sleep!

Rock-a-Bye, Baby

Rock-a-bye, baby, on the treetop,
When the wind blows the cradle will rock;
When the bough breaks the cradle will fall,
Down will come baby, cradle and all.

O Lady Moon

O Lady Moon, your horns point towards the east:
Shine, be increased;
O Lady Moon, your horns point towards the west:
Wane, be at rest.

Christina Rossetti

Star Wish

Star light, star bright,
First star I see tonight,
I wish I may, I wish I might,
Have the wish I wish tonight.

God Bless Me

I see the moon,
And the moon sees me;
God bless the moon,
And God bless me.

What Do the Stars Do?

What do the stars do
Up in the sky,
Higher than the wind can blow
Or the clouds can fly?

Each star in its own glory
Circles, circles still,
As it was lit to shine and set,
And do its Maker's will.

Twinkle, Twinkle, Little Star

Twinkle, twinkle, little star,
How I wonder what you are!
Up above the world so high,
Like a diamond in the sky.

Jane and Ann Taylor

My Bed Is a Boat

My bed is like a little boat;
Nurse helps me in when I embark;
She girds me in my sailor's coat
And starts me in the dark.

At night, I go on board and say
Goodnight to all my friends on shore;
I shut my eyes and sail away
And see and hear no more.

And sometimes things to bed I take,
As prudent sailors have to do:
Perhaps a slice of wedding-cake,
Perhaps a toy or two.

All night across the dark we steer:
But when the day returns at last,
Safe in my room, beside the pier,
I find my vessel fast.

Robert Louis Stevenson

Golden Slumbers

Golden slumbers
Kiss your eyes,
Smiles await you
When you rise.
Sleep little baby,
Don't you cry,
And I will sing a lullaby.

Good Night

Here's a body—there's a bed!
There's a pillow—here's a head!
There's a curtain—here's a light!
There's a puff—and so good night!

Thomas Hood

Index of Titles and First Lines

Index of Authors